THIS BOOK BELONGS TO

CAROL MOORMAN

THE BEST BIRTHDAY

*A Christmas Entertainment
for Children*

THE BEST BIRTHDAY

*A Christmas Entertainment
for Children*

by
GRACE LIVINGSTON HILL

MATTITUCK

Copyright © 1938 by
Grace Livingston Hill

Copyright © 1983 by
Amereon House
All rights reserved

International Standard Book Number 0-89190-404-2

To order contact:
AMEREON HOUSE
the publishing division of
Amereon Ltd.
Box 1200
Mattituck, New York 11952

Manufactured in the United States of America by
The Mad Printers of Mattituck

INTRODUCTION

Grace Livingston Hill was born in Wellsville, New York April 16, 1865, the daughter of the Rev. Charles Montgomery Livingston and Marcia Macdonald Livingston. In her immediate family, there were seven Presbyterian ministers and even her name, Grace, was given her because of its theological meaning. Her mother wrote stories for religious magazines, and her aunt, Isabella Alden ("Pansy"), was a writer of books for juveniles.

Grace was educated at home under private tutors and at the Cincinnati Art School and Elmira College, where she also studied art.

From childhood, Mrs. Hill had loved to write stories and as long as she lived, her mother was her helpful critic. Her aunt, Pansy, had her first story, *The Esselstynes*, published as a surprise when Grace was twelve.

In 1892, Grace Livingston married another Presbyterian minister, the Rev. Thomas Franklin Hill, and they had two daughters, Ruth and Margaret. He died in 1899, and her father immediately thereafter. Now Mrs. Hill was obliged to write to support her children. She conducted a weekly syndicated column in the religious papers, and she continued to write the novels which had begun as a hobby. Of her early days as a writer she said, "The truth is I never did consciously prepare for my literary career, and, furthermore, I have no method at all. Coming from a family of authors, it never came into my mind that preparation was necessary."

She was a tactile, prolific writer, turning out about three books a year. She wrote in the midst of interruptions, without disturbance. For an impressive total of more than 100 books and stories.

A widow for many years, in 1916 Mrs. Hill became Mrs. Flavius J. Lutz. Although she was always reluctant to discuss her second marriage, it was apparently not happy and led eventually to separation — Mrs. Hill was, of course, adamantly opposed to divorce. She lived in Swarthmore, Pennsylvania, in an old stone house, and worked in a second-story room "littered with books and magazines." Until her death at age 82 in 1947, she was active in church work, and spoke frequently before religious groups, traveling to her lecture engagements in a big automobile which she called her only luxury. She refused to charge anything for speaking, and singlehandedly supported a mission Sunday School.

At seventy-five she could pass for sixty, with "quick step, full firm voice, deep laugh, and only slightly grayed hair." In her youth she played tennis and rode horseback, and she never lived a cloistered life, though religion was her chief preoccupation.

In her delightful and charming romances, there remains a constant positive spirit that conquers discouragement, and supports the belief that true love and happiness are born from the worst of trials. Her gift is of understanding — making her characters seem real and her stories true-to-life.

Joanna Paulsen
July 1983

FOREWORD

Down Fairfield Road in Swarthmore, Pa., there is a lovely little old stone church surrounded by a quaint cemetery. It is known as the Old Leiper Church, and has a Sunday School in which I have been working for a good many years.

One Christmas we decided that in place of the usual common-place Christmas tree, and the usual "pieces" recited and sung in honor of Christmas, it would be well to have something that would fix in all our minds the real meaning of Christmas, making plain the prophecies concerning Christ's coming and their fulfillment, and making God's plan of salvation the central thought.

So I chose two young boys to be the leading characters, boys old enough to understand what we were trying to do, young enough to enter into the spirit of the "play," as they called it, earnest enough to care about it and work faithfully, gifted enough to speak clearly and distinctly so that they would gain the instant attention and instant interest of the audience. Then I called in all the rest of the girls and boys who were willing to help us, and we began to build upon this program.

For it was not all written at one sitting. It grew as we began to practise it, and as other girls and boys came into it. The average age of participation was from twelve to fifteen years, though there were some as young as seven and had small parts, and some as old as seventeen.

All of them were interested, and all of them realized that there might be some in their audience who came to die for their sins, or some who had been taught to doubt whether the story of salvation was true, and that it might be in God's plans to use this simple setting forth of proofs to convince some heart and lead someone to accept the Lord Jesus Christ as his personal Saviour.

So, for three consecutive Christmases we have given this story of "The Best Birthday" over again, with the same young actors taking the parts. The actual given names of our young people are used in the text.

And because others have heard about it, and asked to have the program printed, I am putting it into practical form. And we, the young people and I who have been giving it, send greetings and glad Christmas wishes to all who shall care to use it hereafter.

Grace Livingston Hill

THE BEST BIRTHDAY

A group of young people, headed by Joe march up the left aisle, joyously singing the first verse of number 2, PINEBROOK CHORUSES, "Oh, Say But I'm Glad!"

Charlie, walking slowly up the right aisle, watches them wistfully, and meets them just in front of the pulpit as the singing ends.

CHARLIE Say, What makes you kids look so happy? Your faces are just a broad grin.

JOE We are happy! Christmas is coming!

ALL
(except Charlie) Yes! Christmas! Merry Christmas!

CHARLIE Oh, Christmas! What's Christmas? I suppose you kids are going to hang up your stockings, and expect to get jumping-jacks and dolls and a lot of toys that'll be all broken by the next day. You'll maybe have a tree and hang dingle-dangles on it, and eat turkey and lollipops, and be cross and sick the next day. Christmas isn't all it's cracked up to be by a long shot!

JOE Yes, we may hang up our stockings, and get some toys in them. But Christmas brings a better gift than any that can be found in stockings, or on a tree. Christmas brings the best gift of all.

CHARLIE What's that?

JOE The gift of God, which is eternal life! If it hadn't been for Christmas we never could have had the gift at all, and it's the best gift there is.

CHARLIE How do you make that out? What's Christmas got to do with eternal life? Christmas is a pain in the neck!

JOE Christmas is not a pain in the neck! Why, if Jesus had never been born so He could die for us, there wouldn't have been anything but eternal death for

THE BEST BIRTHDAY

us. It had to be somebody who had never sinned who would die for us, you know. Christmas is the grandest day of all the year, except Easter; that's better yet. Christmas is a birthday, too. The best birthday there is!

CHARLIE   Whose birthday?

JOE   The birthday of a King!

CHARLIE   Who d'ya mean? Santa Claus?

JOE   Oh no! Not Santa Claus. He's not real. He's just a play character like a fairy. I mean Jesus, the Son of God. Christmas is Jesus' birthday.

A group of girls at the side, whispering and laughing   (He thought Christmas was Santa Claus' birthday! Isn't that funny? Surely he must know better than that!)

CHARLIE (scowling)   How do you know Christmas is Jesus' birthday?

JOE   The Bible tells us so. His whole story is written there!

CHARLIE   Aw, the Bible! That's just a book. Somebody wrote it out of his head! It's just imagination!

JOE (shaking   No, you're all wrong! "Holy men

his head)	of God spake as they were moved by the Holy Ghost!"
CHARLIE	Where d'ya get that?
JOE	Second Peter, one, twenty-one. Say it kids! (he turns to the other children with him).
ALL (but Charlie)	"For the prophecy came not in old time by the will of man: but holy men of God spake as they were moved by the Holy Ghost."
CHARLIE	What's the Holy Ghost? How could it move them to speak and write?
DOROTHY	The Holy Ghost is not an it! He's a person! He's the same as God. He told the men what to say, just the way the sunshine makes plants grow.
CHARLIE	Aw, that sounds silly! How could He?
JOHN	Maybe it does sound silly to people that don't know Jesus, for the Bible says: "The natural man receiveth not the things of the Spirit of God: for they are foolishness unto him: neither can he know them because they are

THE BEST BIRTHDAY 15

spiritually discerned." (Cor. 2:14)

ANNA It says, too, that the preaching of the cross is to them that perish foolishness; but to those who are saved, it is the power of God (1 Cor. 1:18)

ALBERT Yes, and it says, "If our gospel be hid, it is hid to them that are lost!" (2 Cor. 4:3)

CHARLIE Well, if I ever heard such nonsense! Who is this Jesus, anyway?

PAUL He is the Son of God!

ALBERT He is the Saviour of the world!

ANNA He is God come down to earth!

CHARLIE What would God want to come down to earth for?

JOHN To save us. He had to take on a human body so He could die for us. He is "The Lamb of God which taketh away the sin of the world" (John 1:29)

CHARLIE What would He want to save us for?

ELVIRA Because He loved us.

CHARLIE How do you know that?

ELVIRA	The Bible says so in John three, sixteen. Say it kids!
ALL (except Charlie)	"For God so loved the world that He gave His only begotten Son, that whosoever believeth in Him should not perish, but have everlasting life." (John 3:16)
JOE	We know a song about that! (Joe starts it and all except Charlie sing.) (Tabernacle Hymns No. 2, page 94.) (For God so Loved the World).
CHARLIE	Well save us from what?
ALL (except Charlie shout)	SIN!
CHARLIE	I'm not a sinner! I haven't done anything so very dreadful!
DOROTHY	The Bible says "There is none that doeth good, no not one." (Rom. 3:12)
ANNA	And the Bible says, "All have sinned and come short of the glory of God (Rom. 3:23)
ANGELINE	It's terrible enough not being exactly like God. He wants us to be like Him.

THE BEST BIRTHDAY 17

MARY The Bible says "The wages of sin is death, but the gift of God is eternal life through Jesus Christ our Lord." (Rom. 6:23)

CHARLIE Well, if He calls us sinners, what makes you think He loves us?

MARGARET The Bible says "God commendeth His love toward us in that, while we were yet sinners, Christ died for us." (Rom. 5:8)

EARLE It says, "I have loved thee with an everlasting love, therefore with loving kindness have I drawn thee." (Jer. 31:3)

CHARLIE Well, what's all this got to do with Christmas anyway, and why on earth does it seem to make you so awful happy?

ANGELINE Why, away back, two thousand years ago before Christ was born, God told Abraham that through his seed all the nations of the earth should be blessed. Blessed means happy — and Jesus is the seed promised. And then, about six hundred years before Jesus was born Isaiah told about Him in the Bible. (Isaiah 53) He said He was going to be wounded for our transgressions, He was going to be bruised for our iniquities, that the chastisement of our peace was going to be upon Him, and that with His stripes we were going to be healed. That was a part of the prophecy of how He was to suffer on the cross for our sins. And we are happy because we won't ever have to be punished for our sins.

CHARLIE Do you mean to say the Bible told all about Him before He was born?

ANGELINE Oh yes, and it told a lot more.

ANNA It told how He was to be born, and live and die, and everything about Him. And it all came true, just as it was foretold.

CHARLIE All right. Let's hear it!

JOE Okay, kids, let's begin. What say the prophets? Dorothy you tell him about the first prophecy that a Saviour was going to come.

DOROTHY It was away back in the garden of Eden, after Satan got into the serpent and talked to Eve, and made her believe that it would

THE BEST BIRTHDAY 19

be all right to break God's command and eat the fruit, so she ate it and gave some to Adam. And then they were afraid when they heard God call them, because they knew they had sinned. Then God came and talked to them. He said: "What is this that thou hast done?" and He said to the serpent, "Because thou hast done this thou art cursed above all cattle, and above every beast of the field, and I will put enmity between thee and the woman, and between thy seed and her seed; it shall bruise thy head, (That meant that Jesus, the seed of the woman, would finally kill Satan) and thou shalt bruise his heel." (That meant that Jesus was to be crucified through the acts of Satan.) That is the first prophecy found in the Bible that the Saviour was to be one of the future descendants of Eve. It is found in Genesis 3:15.

JOE What next? Mary, you tell another prophecy.

MARY Isaiah told that Jesus was to be born of a virgin. You find that in

Isaiah 7:14. "Therefore the Lord Himself shall give you a sign; Behold, a virgin shall concieve, and bear a son, and shall call His name Immanuel," which meant, "God with us." That was written seven hundred years before Christ was born.

CHARLIE And did that come true?

MARY It certainly did. You find that in the first chapter of Matthew, verses eighteen to twenty-three. Let's all say them, girls!

VIOLET, RUTH, ROSE, MADELINE, EMMA, MARGARET Now the birth of Jesus Christ was on this wise: When as his mother Mary was espoused to Joseph, before they came together she was found with child of the Holy Ghost.

Then Joseph her husband, being a just man, and not willing to make her a public example, was minded to put her away privily.

But while he thought on these things, behold, the angel of the Lord appeared unto him in a dream, saying, Joseph, thou son of David, fear not to take unto thee Mary thy wife: for that which is conceived in her is of the Holy Ghost.

And she shall bring forth a son, and thou shalt call His name Jesus: for He shall save His people from their sins.

Now all this was done, that it might be fulfilled which was spoken of the Lord by the prophet, saying, Behold a virgin shall be with child, and shall bring forth a son, and they shall call His Immanuel, which being interpreted is "God with us." (Matthew 1:23)

ALBERT Yes, and the prophet Zechariah told beforehand what would happen when He came. He said He would be sold for thirty pieces of silver. You find that in Zechariah eleven, twelve. "And I said unto them, if ye think good, give me my price; and if not forbear. So they weighed for my price thirty pieces of silver."

EARLE In Psalm forty-one, nine it was foretold how He would be betrayed by Judas, one of His own disciples. Judas was the one who was paid the thirty pieces of silver by the chief priests. The Psalm says, "Yea, mine own familiar friend, in whom I trusted, which did eat of my bread, hath lifted up his heel against me."

PAUL Yes, and in John thirteen, eighteen, Jesus reminded them of that. He said, "I speak not of you all. I know whom I have chosen: but that the scriptures might be fulfilled, "He that eateth bread with me hath lifted up his heel against me."

CLARENCE Zechariah told, too, how Christ was going to be forsaken by His disciples. Chapter thirteen, verse seven. "Awake, O sword, against my shepherd, and against the man that is my fellow, saith the Lord of hosts: smite the shepherd and the sheep shall be scattered."

MADELINE That was fulfilled in Matthew twenty-six, thirty-one. "Then saith Jesus unto them, All ye shall be offended because of me this night, for it is written, I will smite the shepherd and the sheep shall be scattered abroad."

ERNEST Verse fifty-six in that same chap

THE BEST BIRTHDAY

ter in Matthew shows the fulfillment, too. "But all this was done that the scriptures of the prophets might be fulfilled: "Then all the disciples forsook Him and fled."

CLARENCE Psalm thirty-five, eleven told that He was going to be accused by false witnesses: It says: "False witnesses did rise up; they laid to my charge things that I knew not."

ALBERT Yes, and that was fulfilled in Matthew twenty-six, verses fifty-nine to sixty-one. "Now the chief priests and elders, and all the council, sought false witnesses against Jesus, to put Him to death, but found none. Yea, though many false witnesses came, yet found they none. At last came two false witnesses and said, this fellow said, I am able to destroy the temple of God and to build it in three days." They thought He meant the building where they worshipped but He meant the temple of His body, looking forward to His death and resurrection.

ANNA Well Isaiah said, in chapter fifty-three, the seventh verse, that He was going to be silent before His accusers. "He was oppressed, and He was afflicted, yet He opened not His mouth. He is brought as a lamb to the slaughter, and as a sheep before her shearers is dumb, so He openeth not His mouth.

PAUL That was fulfilled in Matthew twenty-seven, thirteen and fourteen. "Then said Pilate unto Him, hearest thou not how many things they witness against thee? And He answered them never a word; insomuch that the governor marvelled greatly."

DOROTHY In Isaiah the fiftieth chapter and the sixth verse, it said He was going to be spit upon and scourged. It says: "I gave my back to the smiters, and my cheeks to them that plucked off the hair. I hid not my face from shame and spitting." And that was fulfilled in Matthew twenty-seven, twenty-six: "Then released he Barabbas unto them: and when he had scourged Jesus, he delivered Him to be crucified." And in chapter twenty-six, verse sixty-seven, "Then they did spit in His face and buffeted Him."

ANGELINE Psalm twenty-two, eighteen, told how His garments were going to be parted. It says: "And they parted my garments among them, and cast lots upon my vesture." And it tells in Matthew twenty-seven, thirty-five how that was fulfilled. "And they crucified Him, and parted his garments, casting lots: that it might be fulfilled which was spoken by the prophet, They parted my garments among them, and upon my vesture did they cast lots."

EMMA In Psalm twenty-two, seven and eight it says: "All they that see me laugh me to scorn; they shoot out the lip, they shake the head saying, He trusted on the Lord that He would deliver Him: let Him deliver Him, seeing He delighted in Him."

ALMA That was fulfilled in Matthew twenty-seven, forty-one to forty-three: "Likewise also the chief priests mocking Him, with the scribes and elders, said, He saved others: Himself He cannot save. If He be the King of Israel, let Him now come down from the cross, and we will believe Him. He trusted in God; let Him deliver Him now, if He will have Him: for He said, I am the Son of God."

JUNIOR Psalm sixty-nine, twenty-one, says: "They gave me also gall for my meat; and in my thirst they gave me vinegar to drink."

ALBERT They did that when He was on the cross. Don't you remember Matthew twenty-seven, forty-eight? "And straightway one of them ran, and took a sponge, and filled it with vinegar, and put it on a reed and gave Him to drink."

JOE It was foretold in Psalm twenty-two, one, how God was going to forsake Him:"My God, my God, why hast Thou forsaken me?" And in Matthew twenty-seven, forty-six it tells how that was fulfilled: "And about the ninth hour Jesus cried with a loud voice, saying, Eli, Eli, lama sabachthani?" that is to say, My

THE BEST BIRTHDAY

God, my God why hast Thou forsaken me?"

ANTHONY It was said, too, that He was to die with wicked men. Isaiah fifty-three, twelve: "And He was numbered with the transgressors, and He bare the sin of many, and made intercession for the transgressors."

ANNA It tells how that was fulfilled, in Luke twenty-three, thirty-two and thirty-three: "And there were also two other malefactors, let with Him to be put to death. And when they were to come to the place, which is called Calvary, there they crucified Him, and the malefactors, one on the right hand, and the other on the left."

SAMUEL Oh, yes, you find that in Psalm thirty-four, twenty, that His bones were not to be broken. "He keepeth all His bones, not one of them is broken." Was that fulfilled too?

PAUL Oh, yes, you find that in John nineteen, thirty-two and thirty-three: "Then came the soldiers and brake the legs of the first and of the other which was crucified with Him. But when they came to Jesus, and saw that He was dead already, they brake not His legs."

CLARENCE It says in Isaiah fifty-three, nine, that Jesus was appointed to be buried with the wicked, but that He would be with the rich because he had done no violence; and He would have been buried in the potter's field with the two thieves, only a rich man, Joseph of Arimathaea, begged His body of Pilate and buried Him in his own garden. You find that in Luke twenty-three, verses fifty to fifty-three.

CHARLIE Well, but say, did all these people know all about these prophecies beforehand?

ERNEST I'll say they did. It was all written in the sacred books, and the whole nation was expecting a Messiah to come some day who would save the people from their sins. Every household was hoping that the child would be born in their home.

THE BEST BIRTHDAY

CHARLIE Then I don't see why they crucified Him.

CLARENCE They didn't recognize Him. Perhaps they didn't listen to the prophecy when it was read in their synagogues. Perhaps they didn't realize He was to be like that. They expected a great king with a jeweled crown and ermine robes. One born in a palace, who would free them from their enemies and make them all wealthy. They didn't expect him to be born in a manger, and most of them didn't want the kind of life he offered.

JOE Yes, you see the people wanted money and power instead of eternal life and goodness . But there were a lot of other prophecies. You haven't told half of them. There were several about his resurrection from the dead.

ARTHUR Oh yes, Psalm sixteen, ten, says: "For thou wilt not leave my soul in hell" — that means the place of the dead — ; "neither wilt thou suffer thine Holy One to see corruption." This is a prophecy that the Lord's body

	should only remain in the grave three days, because in that land a dead body begins to decay after three days.
SAMUEL	Yes, and Acts two, twenty-five to thirty-one call that to mind. It quotes that verse and says that David, being a prophet, understood that God would raise up Christ from the dead. And it goes on to say: "He seeing this before spake of the resurrection of Christ, that His soul was not left in hell neither His flesh did see corruption." And I've heard that even lawyers say that there is more proof of Christ's resurrection than of any other fact in history.
CHARLIE	Well that certainly is interesting!
JOE	Yes, isn't it? And then, He's coming again, you know!
CHARLIE	Coming again? What makes you think that?
JOE	The Bible says so. In Acts one, eleven: "This same Jesus, which is taken up from you into heaven, shall so come in like manner as ye have seen Him go into heaven."

THE BEST BIRTHDAY

	That's what the angels said.
DOROTHY	Jesus Himself said He was coming. You find it in John fourteen, three and four: "I'll go to prepare a place for you. And if I go and prepare a place for you, I will come again, and receive you unto myself, that where I am, there ye may be also."
JOE	Now let's all say first Thessalonians four, sixteen to eighteen.
ALL (except Charlie)	"For the Lord Himself shall descend from heaven with a shout, with the voice of the archangel, and with the trump of God: and the dead in Christ shall rise first: then we which are alive and remain shall be caught up together with them in the clouds, to meet the Lord in the air: and so shall we ever be with the Lord. Wherefore comfort one another with these words."
ANTHONY	Joy and I know a song about that!
JOE	All right, sing it now.
JOY AND ANTHONY SING:	I'll Be So Glad.

CHARLIE   Say, that's great! But that's a long time ago all that was written! A lot of years have rolled by, and nothing has happened. I guess it doesn't amount to anything nowadays, does it?

DOROTHY   Oh, the Bible even prophesies that people would talk like that. You find it in second Peter, third chapter. "There shall come in the last days scoffers, walking after their own lusts, and saying, where is the promise of His coming? For since the fathers fell asleep, all things continue as they were from the beginning of the creation. But, beloved, be not ignorant of this one thing, that one day is with the Lord as a thousand years, and a thousand years as one day. The Lord is not slack concerning His promise, as some men count slackness; but is longsuffering to usward, not willing that any should perish, but that all should come to repentance.

JOE   Jesus Christ is the same, yesterday, today, and forever, and God has never broken a promise

THE BEST BIRTHDAY

yet. Sing it kids!

Joe starts it and they all sing number 235 in "Tabernacle Hymns No. 2" "Yesterday, To-Day, Forever, Jesus is the same." (Sing only chorus if preferred.)

CHARLIE	Say, I'd like to get in on this thing myself. How do you do it?
JOE	Just believe on the Lord Jesus Christ and thou shalt be saved.
CHARLIE	Don't ya havta pay anything?
JOE	Not a cent! It's a gift!
ALL (except Charlie) sing	"Jesus Paid It All," Number 288, "Tabernacle Hymns No. 2."
CHARLIE	You mean I could be saved that easy?
JOE	Sure you could! It's all been done for you! John five, twenty-four. Say it kids!
All (but Charlie) recite in unison:	"Verily, verily, I say unto you, He that heareth my word and believeth on Him that sent me, hath everlasting life, and shall not come into condemnation: but is passed from death unto life."
CHARLIE	But wouldn't I have to be judged for my sins!

JOE	No! Jesus has already been judged for your sins, and the sins of the whole world! Second Corinthians five, twenty-one. Say it, kids!
ALL (except Charlie)	"For He hath made Him to be sin for us, Who knew no sin: that we might be made the righteousness of God in Him."
JOE	And first John two, two!
ALL (except Charlie)	"And He is the propitiation for our sins; and not for ours only, but also for the sins of the whole world."
CHARLIE	Then why isn't everybody saved?
ARTHUR	They won't all believe. It says in John three, eighteen: "He that believeth on Him is not condemned, but he that believeth not is condemned already, because he hath not believed on the name of the only begotten Son of God."
CHARLIE	Then I'll believe right now!
JOE	That's grand!

(They shake hands.)

THE BEST BIRTHDAY

JOE (turning to them all)	Let's all sing! (He starts.)
ALL sing (with bowed heads)	"Just as I am without one plea, But that Thy blood was shed for me, And that Thou bidst me come to Thee, O Lamb of God, I come, I come!"
CHOIR (in distance sing)	"Ring the Bells of heaven, There is joy today, For a soul returneth from the wild"
	or
	"Joy, joy, joy, There is joy in heaven with the angels, Joy, joy, joy, for the Prodigal returns."
CHARLIE	Now I can sing with you, for I am happy too!
All sing as they march to their seats:	"I'm so Happy," Number 104 in New Pinebrook Songs.